SAVING THE
SEA
TURTLE

LOUISE SPILSBURY

CHERITON
CHILDREN'S BOOKS

Published in 2023 by **Cheriton Children's Books**
PO Box 7258, Bridgnorth WV16 9ET, UK

© 2023 Cheriton Children's Books

First Edition

Author: Louise Spilsbury
Designer: Paul Myerscough
Editor: Jane Brooke
Proofreader: Tracey Kelly
Consultant: David Hawksett, BSc

Picture credits: Cover: Shutterstock/Bruna Boettge. Inside: p1: Shutterstock/Rich Carey; pp4-5: Shutterstock/Michael Smith ITWP; pp6-7: Shutterstock/Laverne Nash; p7b: Shutterstock/Agami Photo Agency; p7t: Shutterstock/Hadot 760; p8b: Shutterstock/Coulanges; pp10-11: Shutterstock/Rich Carey; pp12-13: Shutterstock/Rich Carey; p13b: Shutterstock/Rich Carey; p13t: Shutterstock/Aleksei Alekhin; pp14-15: Shutterstock/Rich Carey; pp16-17: Shutterstock/Stockphoto-graf; p17b: Shutterstock/AJP; p17t: Shutterstock/AJP; pp18-19: Shutterstock/Tatyana Blinova; p19b: Shutterstock/Oksana Golubeva; pp20-21: Shutterstock/Vkilikov; p21b: Shutterstock/AliveGK; p21c: Shutterstock/Tomas Kotouc; p21t: Shutterstock/Chase Dekker; pp22-23: Shutterstock/GracePhotos; p23b: Shutterstock/Lassedesignen; p23t: Shutterstock/Lassedesignen; pp24-25: Shutterstock/Khairul Fikiri Osman; p25b: Shutterstock/JB Manning; pp26-27: Shutterstock/Agami Photo Agency; p27b: Shutterstock/Ricky Ashmun; p27c: Shutterstock/Igor Batenev; p27t: Shutterstock/Elvin A. Santana; pp28-29: Shutterstock/Shane Myers Photography; p28b: Shutterstock/Curraheeshutter; p29b: Shutterstock/Elena Elisseeva; p29t: Shutterstock/Elena Elisseeva; pp30-31: Shutterstock/Richard Whitcombe; p31b: Shutterstock/Tunatura; pp32-33: Shutterstock/Ed Jenkins; p32b: Shutterstock/Stephan Kerkhofs; p33b: Shutterstock/Drew McArthur; p33t: Shutterstock/Charlie Reaney; pp34-35: Shutterstock/Rich Carey; p34b: Shutterstock/Digitalskillet; p34t: Shutterstock/Digitalskillet; p35c: Shutterstock/Larina Marina; pp36-37: Shutterstock/Yoye Jantapoon; p36b: Shutterstock/Elliotte Rusty Harold; pp38-39: Shutterstock/Danny Ye; p39b: Shutterstock/Tomas Kotouc; p39t: Shutterstock/Rich Carey; pp40-41: Shutterstock/Scubadesign; p41b: Shutterstock/Allensima; p41t: Shutterstock/Allensima; p42: Shutterstock/W Underwater; p43: Shutterstock/Steklo; p44t: Shutterstock/Trevor Charles Graham; p45b: Shutterstock/KT Stock photos.

Printed in China

Publisher's Note: The information in the Kids on a Mission features in this book are suggestions for actions that children can take to help protect endangered animals, based on extensive research by the author and consultant. The email addresses and the children featured in the photographs are for illustrative purposes only.

Please visit our website,
www.cheritonchildrensbooks.com,
to see more of our high-quality books.

CONTENTS

SEA TURTLES IN DANGER

Sea turtles are one of the oldest creatures on the planet. There were sea turtles on Earth more than 100 million years ago. They even shared the world with dinosaurs until they became **extinct** around 65 million years ago. Sea turtles have a heavy shell and short, wide legs.

THE BIGGEST THREAT

Adult sea turtles can be eaten by orcas, or killer whales. They can also be eaten by sharks, seals, and crocodiles. However, humans are by far the biggest threat to sea turtles. In the past, hundreds of thousands of sea turtles were hunted for food. Today, people still hunt sea turtles, but they also now destroy the animals' beach and ocean homes. Sea turtles become trapped and die in fishing nets and lines. **Climate change** and ocean **pollution** also put them in danger.

"We have it within our power to protect these animals ... but all those who have a hand in shaping their future need to work together to do so."

Alison Gunn, Fauna & Flora International (FFI)

▲ Sea turtles look incredibly beautiful and graceful when gliding through the oceans.

HELP THE SEA TURTLE!

There is still hope for the sea turtle, and it is not too late to save it. People everywhere have heard the sea turtle's call for help. And they are making it their mission to help these amazing animals survive. In this book, we'll learn about the sea turtle and why it is in danger. We'll discover what people are doing to help sea turtles and how they have built a career in conservation. We'll find out how kids everywhere can make it their mission to help save the sea turtle. And we'll learn how you could make a career in conservation your mission. Feeling mission-ready? Then read on!

SEA TURTLES NEED OUR HELP

There is a real danger that if we do not do more to protect sea turtles, one day they may be gone forever. **Conservationists** are working to do all they can to save the remaining sea turtles on Earth, and they need our help.

5

CHAPTER ONE

MEET THE SEA TURTLE

Sea turtles are amazing animals. They come onto land to have babies, but they spend most of their lives underwater. Sea turtles have unique features that help them survive in the oceans.

BIG AND SMALL

Sea turtles vary greatly in size. Kemp's ridley is the smallest. It measures 28 inches (70 cm) long. It weighs up to 100 pounds (45 kg). In comparison, the leatherback can be up to 6 feet (180 cm) long. It weighs 1,100 pounds (500 kg). That's more than 10 times heavier than Kemp's ridley sea turtle!

TOP TO BOTTOM

Most sea turtles have hard, bony outer shells. Inside are light, spongy bones. They help the sea turtles float. Sea turtles have long flippers instead of feet. They use their big, strong front flippers like paddles to move through the water. They use the smaller back flippers to help them steer.

SEA SURVIVORS

Sea turtles are a type of **reptile**. Reptiles breathe air. Sea turtles usually swim to the ocean surface to breathe every few minutes. However, they can stay underwater for several hours when resting or sleeping. To do so, they slow their heart rate. Their heart can beat just once every 9 minutes to save oxygen.

DEEP DIVERS

The sea turtle's ability to hold its breath helps it dive deep under the water to find food. Most turtles can dive to depths of up to 960 feet (290 m). However, the leatherback sea turtle can dive to depths of more than 3,000 feet (1,000 m)!

TURTLE TEARS

Turtles cry—but not because they are sad! Sea turtles drink seawater. Seawater is salty, and if too much salt remains inside a turtle's body, it would make it sick. To avoid that, sea turtles empty the salt from their eyes. That is why they look as if they are crying.

In a Group

Scientists group animals to help them classify, or order, them. Sea turtles are grouped into two families. *Cheloniidae* includes all sea turtles with hard shells, such as the loggerhead sea turtle. Leatherback sea turtles are a separate *Dermochelyidae* family. The turtles in that group have a leathery shell instead of a hard shell.

loggerhead sea turtle

leatherback sea turtle

WHERE SEA TURTLES LIVE

Sea turtles live in open water but also visit land along the coasts to have their young in areas called nesting sites. Sea turtles can be found in the middle of the oceans and in shallow **seagrass** beds at the edge of the water. They can also be found around colorful **coral reefs** and on sandy beaches.

MAGNIFICENT SEVEN

There are seven different types of sea turtle. They are the:
- Green sea turtle
- Hawksbill sea turtle
- Loggerhead sea turtle
- Olive ridley sea turtle
- Kemp's ridley sea turtle
- Flatback sea turtle
- Leatherback sea turtle

▼ Leatherback sea turtles can survive in colder waters than other sea turtles. That allows them to feed in waters nearer to the North and South Poles. However, they come ashore in tropical areas to lay their eggs.

HOME, SWEET HOME

Most types of sea turtles can be found in oceans all over the world. They usually prefer warmer tropical and subtropical waters. The tropics are areas of the Earth that lie roughly in an imaginary belt around the middle of the planet that is known as the equator. These areas on or near the equator are warmer than elsewhere on Earth. Kemp's ridley sea turtles are found mainly in the Gulf of Mexico. The flatback sea turtle is mainly found around northern Australia and southern Papua New Guinea.

JAPAN

CAPE VERDE

MYANMAR

MEXICO
EL SALVADOR

PHILIPPINES

INDIA

NICARAGUA

SRI LANKA

MALAYSIA

COSTA RICA

SAO TOME
AND PRINCIPE

BANGLADESH

ECUADOR

OMAN

INDONESIA

CONGO

KEY
Where sea turtles are found
Where sea turtle nesting sites are most threatened

TURTLE TRAVELERS

Most sea turtles do not stay in one place. Some sea turtles travel a very long way to find food or a beach on which to lay their eggs. These impressive trips are called migrations. One female leatherback sea turtle is known to have taken a trip of more than 12,000 miles (19,000 km)! It traveled across the Pacific Ocean from Indonesia to the northwest coast of the United States.
Sea turtles have a special **sense** that helps them detect the **magnetic field** of Earth. That acts as a guide to tell them which direction to travel.

HIGH SEAS, HIGH RISKS

The fact that most sea turtles have long migrations puts them under threat. The routes they take often cause them to travel through areas of the ocean that belong to different countries. They also swim in areas of remote, or faraway, oceans that are not owned by any country. These areas are called high seas. When they swim there, sea turtles are at risk because they may pass through places where there are no laws to protect them.

WHY SHOULD WE HELP THE SEA TURTLE?

Sea turtles are incredibly important animals. In fact, sea turtles are a "keystone species." That means that they are a very important part of their **environment**. It means that they are also important to other wildlife and people, too.

A BALANCING ACT

Sea turtles help keep ocean life in balance. For example, leatherback sea turtles eat a lot of jellyfish. That controls the amount of jellyfish in the ocean. If leatherbacks were to disappear, there would be many more jellyfish. Jellyfish eat fish larvae, or babies. If there were too many jellyfish, there would be fewer fish babies and fewer fish in the sea. Many sea turtle shells also provide some small **organisms** with a home. Barnacles, **algae**, and even small crabs can live on the surface of a sea turtle's shell.

HELPING HABITATS

Sea turtles help ocean **habitats**, too. For example, many fish and shellfish live in seagrass meadows. Seagrass needs sea turtles to grow properly. Without sea turtles, seagrass becomes overgrown and starts to rot. When sea turtles feed on seagrass, it becomes healthier. That then gives other animals a larger area in which to live and feed. Humans also benefit, because they eat many of the animals that live in seagrass. Seagrass meadows also help people by protecting coastlines from storms and **erosion**.

◀ If there were no sea turtles to keep seagrass meadows healthy, the animals' ecosystem would suffer.

What Is an
Ecosystem?

An ecosystem is a group of natural parts that all work together for a purpose. Ecosystems include nonliving things such as water, sunshine, and air. These are called abiotic factors. Ecosystems also include living things such as plants and animals. These are called biotic factors. The living things in an ecosystem depend on the abiotic factors in the ecosystem to survive. Every part of the ecosystem has an important part to play. A healthy ecosystem has many different plants and animals living together. If any part of that ecosystem changes or is damaged, the other parts are affected, too.

SEA TURTLE DINNERS

Sea turtles spend most of their day resting and feeding, and then resting again. Different sea turtles eat different types of food.

ON THE MENU

Most sea turtles are omnivores. That means they eat both plants and animals. They eat different types of plants, including algae, seaweed, and seagrasses. They eat a variety of animals, including jellyfish, squid, barnacles, sponges, and **sea anemones**. The adult green sea turtle eats only plants. However, baby green sea turtles eat fish eggs, **mollusks**, and **crustaceans**.

FINDING FOOD

Sea turtle eyes are **adapted** to see very well under the waves. That helps them find food. Sea turtles also have an excellent sense of smell. That helps them locate food in murky or dark water when they are hungry.

MIGHTY MOUTHS

Most sea turtles have very sharp beaks and strong jaws. They use them to crush their food. Sea turtles also have spikes in their throats. Sea turtles spit out any water they take in while feeding. The spikes keep food from slipping back out of their mouth when they do so.

TEARING AND MUNCHING

Leatherbacks don't have a beak. Their mouthparts work like scissors to grasp and swallow their jellyfish food.

PEOPLE ON A MISSION

Sea turtles are under threat, but they are not alone. Many people around the planet have made it their mission to help sea turtles. Some have chosen to work in conservation. They devote their lives to working to protect these beautiful animals.

PEOPLE ON THE GROUND

Wildlife managers, rangers, and officers are conservationists who work in places where the sea turtle lives. They help protect its home and monitor its numbers. They may rescue and treat injured sea turtles before they release them back into the wild. Wildlife technicians collect data, or information, on wildlife and habitats. They often work alongside a wildlife manager. Public educators and outreach specialists educate people about sea turtles.

Observing sea turtles in ▶ their natural environment helps people learn more about these animals.

PEOPLE IN OFFICES

People who work in offices in conservation organizations perform a variety of jobs. They use information from scientists to develop guidance to help others carry out conservation actions. For example, they work with governments and companies to develop ways of protecting coastal areas where sea turtles live. There are also charities in which people work hard to raise money to save sea turtles. **Communications** and public relations experts help organizations raise awareness about sea turtles.

PEOPLE IN THE LAB

Zoologists and wildlife technicians are scientists who work in zoos or labs. They have a very important job to do. They study sea turtles in detail to learn more about their lives and needs. The scientists can use this information to advise conservationists about the best ways to help the animals in the wild.

MAKE IT YOUR MISSION

You can help sea turtles and other endangered animals by taking action and planning a career in conservation. Here's how:

1. In this book, you'll discover what actions kids on a mission can take to help sea turtles. Use them to inspire your own actions to rescue sea turtles.
2. You'll also discover some of the careers people on a mission have in sea turtle conservation. As you read about each one, think about whether that career in conservation might suit you.
3. At the end of this book, you'll find a guide to how to build a career in conservation. Check it out to discover how you can make saving animals your life mission.

PEOPLE EVERYWHERE

We can all play our part in helping the sea turtle. We can raise money to save sea turtles. We can learn about threats the animals face. We can share this knowledge with our friends and family. We can join organizations that help sea turtles.

CHAPTER TWO

HOMES UNDER THREAT

Sea turtles rely on healthy, undisturbed habitats to survive. Unfortunately, some of the habitats where they live, feed, and have their young are under threat. That puts sea turtles in danger, too.

BEACHES UNDER THREAT

Sea turtles come onto quiet, sandy beaches to lay their eggs. However, people are building tourist resorts or homes on or near those beaches. They drive vehicles across the beaches. As well as building on the beaches, lights from roads and buildings confuse baby sea turtles that hatch from, or break out of, the eggs inside the nests. Lights can make them head away from the sea, instead of toward it. Vehicles flatten and firm the sand. That makes it too hard for female sea turtles to dig nests. Sea walls and jetties change the way that waves wash onto shores. That can cause the erosion or destruction of entire sections of beach.

HARMING HOMES

Other sea turtle habitats are being destroyed and put under threat. Many sea turtles feed around coral reefs and seagrass beds. However, they are being damaged or even destroyed by human activities. For example, tourists and fishermen damage coral reefs. Careless divers and snorkelers break pieces off the reefs. Boat anchors are dragged across them. Badly driven boats crash into reefs. Oil spills and pollution also harm coral reefs. Oil spills happen when oil pipelines break, big oil tanker ships sink, or drilling operations go wrong. Sewage dumped in the sea is one example of pollution that affects coral reefs.

SOMEWHERE SAFE TO LIVE

To help protect sea turtles, conservationists have set up **marine reserves**. They are areas in which sea turtle habitats should be safe from threats. Marine reserves are monitored by people working in sea turtle conservation, who try and keep the sea turtles living and feeding there safe.

◀ Sea turtles thrive when they can lay eggs on clean beaches and swim in unpolluted waters.

Kids on a Mission

@seaturtlericky_2007

To save sea turtles, I have asked my family to choose products that won't harm the oceans when they are flushed down our toilets or washed into drains from our sinks.

*"People think ... 'how do we clean up the ocean,' and that's the wrong question. The question is, how do we stop **befouling** it in the first place?"*

Ellie Moss, ocean expert

SPOTLIGHT ON SEAGRASS

Seagrasses are marine plants with long, green grasslike leaves. They grow in thick meadows. Seagrasses provide protection and food for many different ocean animals. Seagrass meadows are very important habitats for many sea turtles.

MANY DANGERS

Today, there are a number of threats to seagrass meadows. Farm chemicals such as **fertilizers** wash off the land and into water. These cause algae to grow and spread quickly. These **algal blooms** block sunlight. Seagrasses die without light. Dirt washes into the water as land is cleared for farms and building sites. That covers the seagrass and blocks sunlight. People also dig up seagrass meadows to use the land for building or farming. Boat anchors and propellers can also destroy areas of seagrass.

▲ This area of ocean is covered with algal bloom.

LOSING OUT

Every year, more and more seagrass is lost. When seagrass is under threat, so too, are sea turtles. Adult green sea turtles spend most of their time feeding in seagrass meadows. An adult green sea turtle can eat about 4.5 pounds (2 kg) of seagrass each day. Without the food and shelter that seagrass meadow habitats provide, the green sea turtles are in trouble.

PEOPLE ON A MISSION: SEA TURTLE SUPPORT

Conservationists and wildlife managers monitor seagrass beds across the world to track any changes in seagrass health. They may also get involved with rebuilding damaged seagrass beds. They do that by planting seeds or seedlings that have been grown in **aquariums**. They also sometimes plant adult seagrasses that have been grown in other, healthier meadows.

Wildlife policy analysts and wildlife consultants work with governments and industries to encourage the use of good environmental practices.

For example, they ask farmers to help seagrass habitats by limiting the amount of fertilizers and **pesticides** they use. They work with governments to make regulations, or rules, that keep industries from dumping dangerous waste down drains.

Public education and outreach specialists work with local communities to educate them about the threats to seagrass habitats and sea turtles. They encourage people to be careful when boating, for example, by going more slowly and avoiding shallow areas.

Seagrass is the main food eaten by green ▶ sea turtles. It is estimated that almost 30 percent of seagrass meadows have died since the late nineteenth century.

LIVING NEAR THE SEA TURTLE

Many different animals live in the oceans. Sadly, some of these amazing creatures are endangered too.

THE DUGONG

Dugongs are large mammals that live in tropical coastal areas. Mammals are animals that give birth to live young and feed their babies with milk from their bodies. Dugongs can grow up to almost 10 feet (3 m) long and weigh up to 1,100 pounds (500 kg). They eat up to 90 pounds (40 kg) of seagrass every day. Their flat mouths are turned downward to make it easier to eat seagrass from the seafloor. Dugongs are under threat from habitat loss, boat strikes, and bycatch. Bycatch is ocean animals accidentally caught in fishing nets that are supposed to catch only fish.

THE BLUE WHALE

The blue whale is the largest animal on Earth. It weighs up to 200 tons (181 mt). Its heart is as big as a Volkswagen Beetle car! Blue whales are threatened by habitat loss and ocean pollution. They can be injured or killed when ships hit them and by becoming entangled in fishing gear.

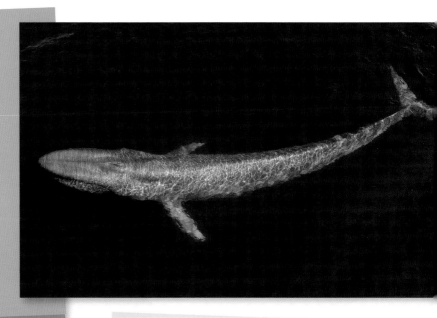

THE GREAT HAMMERHEAD SHARK

The great hammerhead shark is named for its unique hammer-shaped head. This magnificent fish can grow up to 20 feet (6.1 m) long. It can weigh 990 pounds (450 kg). Great hammerheads hunt stingrays and other fish on the ocean floor. Fishing boats catch great hammerhead sharks and sell their huge fins for a lot of money.

THE HECTOR'S DOLPHIN

Hector's dolphins are less than 4 feet (1.2 m) long. Today, there are fewer than 7,000 left in the wild. They are found only in shallow waters along the coast of New Zealand's North Island. They often become entangled in fishing nets or lines. They are also struck by boats.

21

CHAPTER THREE

UNDER THREAT FROM HUNTING

Poaching is the illegal killing or capture of animals. Poachers hunt sea turtles and collect their eggs for food. They also kill sea turtles for their beautiful shells.

SHELL HUNTERS

Some sea turtles are targeted for their shells. The hawksbill sea turtle's beautiful shell is one reason why it is endangered. Poachers kill the sea turtle, and its shell is made into jewelry and other products. They are sold to tourists as "tortoiseshell." Tourists who buy the products on vacation often don't know that they are helping to cause the loss of an endangered species.

The beautiful shell of ▶ the hawksbill sea turtle is highly sought after.

"They are being eaten by people who don't know the value of turtles."

Abdala Ali, fisherman in Watamu, Kenya

HUNTED FOR FOOD

Poaching of sea turtles from their nests for their meat and especially the eggs is a huge problem. The turtle eggs are usually sold to restaurants, where people eat them. Green sea turtles are also poached for their calipee. That is green body fat, which is used in turtle soup. For many poor people living by coasts, selling sea turtle eggs is their only source of income. Without it, they would not be able to feed their families.

AGAINST THE LAW

The illegal wildlife **trade** is the illegal trade of wild plants and animals. This multibillion-dollar business is said to be worth $50 to $150 billion dollars a year. The sea turtle is just one of its victims. The illegal trade of sea turtle eggs, meat, and shells is a major threat to the animals' survival.

Kids on a Mission

@elijahs_earth_choice

I was shocked to read about sea turtle poaching. I will make sure I never buy products that have been made from sea turtle parts. I've told my friends, too.

POACHING

People have hunted sea turtles for thousands of years. Sea turtle meat and eggs were important foods for people living along tropical coasts for centuries. At first, people hunted sea turtles and eggs only to get enough to eat. However, by the sixteenth century, sea turtles were being caught and traded around the world, and not only for food. Combs made of hawksbill sea turtle shells were a popular fashion item during the nineteenth century. Sea turtles were an easy target, because they drifted on the surface of the sea. Sailors could easily spear them. Soon, sea turtle numbers began to decline.

STEALING EGGS

Today, people search the beaches at night for sea turtle nests. They often poke the ground with long sticks to find eggs. When they find a nest, they dig it up and steal all of the eggs. Some turtle eggs are still eaten near where they are found. Most are sold to traders, who take the eggs to cities. There, they are sold in markets and restaurants. Some are traded around the world. At some beaches, poachers destroy more than 90 percent of sea turtle nests.

Trading sea turtle ▶ eggs is illegal. However, each year, poachers raid sea turtle nests, take their eggs, and sell them.

PEOPLE ON A MISSION: PATROL AND EDUCATE

Wildlife rangers and officers work in different ways to protect sea turtles and their nests. They patrol the beaches day and night. They watch out for poachers. If they catch poachers who have already collected eggs, they make them hand over the eggs. They are then buried in the sand again. During a patrol, officers search for information about sea turtle nests. The officers check for signs of sea turtles, such as flipper prints in the sand. They record their findings.

Wildlife officers also use new technology to help them. For example, they hide 3-D (three-dimensional) printed sea turtle eggs inside nests. The fake eggs have **Global Positioning System (GPS)** devices inside. If the spy eggs are taken by poachers, they can be tracked. The information can lead to the capture and arrest of people in the illegal wildlife trade.

Some officers work with local people to find alternative ways to earn money. Some former sea turtle egg poachers now work as wildlife rangers who patrol beaches. Officers also encourage local people to become involved with **sustainable** tourism. That makes the sea turtles worth more to communities alive than dead.

▲ Wildlife officers mark and watch nesting sites to protect sea turtle eggs from poachers.

TINY TURTLES

Female sea turtles can lay hundreds of eggs in one nesting season. But as few as one in 1,000 of the **hatchlings** that come from these eggs survive to adulthood. When humans steal the eggs and disturb or damage nesting beaches, sea turtle **populations** are at risk.

FLIPPER SHOVELS

A female sea turtle returns to the beach where she was born to lay her eggs. She comes ashore at night and uses her back flippers as shovels to dig a hole about 30 inches (80 cm) deep. She lays up to 110 eggs in this nest. They are each about the size of a ping-pong ball.

HIDING THE NEST

After she has laid all her eggs, the female fills the hole with sand. Then, she brushes the sand left and right with her flippers to hide the nest.

ESCAPING THE EGGS

Two months after the eggs were laid, the babies chip their way out. They use a sharp egg "tooth" to break open their egg. The egg tooth falls off soon after the babies hatch. Then, it can take several days for the hatchlings to dig themselves out of the nest.

BEACH RACE

Hatchlings wait until night to leave the nest. They do this to avoid daytime predators and heat. Predators are animals that hunt and eat other animals. Hatchlings follow the moonlight that **reflects** off the sea to find their way. They move as quickly as they can to avoid predators such as crabs, foxes, and birds.

INTO THE OCEAN

When the hatchlings get to the water, they swim very quickly. They have to get to deep water as fast as they can. There are a lot of hungry fish in the shallows that try to catch the hatchlings.

27

CHAPTER FOUR

CLIMATE CHANGE THREATS

We know that because of climate change, our planet is experiencing more extreme weather patterns. That is having a significant impact on habitats, humans, and wildlife such as sea turtles.

Climate change poses a ▶ real threat to the survival of sea turtles and their habitat.

WHAT IS CLIMATE CHANGE?

Climate change is a change in temperature or weather in an area over a long period of time. Climate change has always happened slowly throughout Earth's history, due to natural factors such as changes in the sun and **geological** activity. However, the climate change we are experiencing today is largely caused by human activities. These include burning **fossil fuels**, which releases gases into Earth's **atmosphere**. These gases circle the planet like a blanket, causing it to heat up.

▲ Oil drilled from beneath the ocean is a type of fossil fuel. When it is burned to make heat or power, gases are released that contribute to climate change.

"... their (sea turtles) existence on this planet is at risk due to human activities, including climate change."

Connie Merigo, Rescue Department Manager at the New England Aquarium

Kids on a Mission

@join_jen_4_earth

My family car shares with another family whenever we can. We share rides to school. I'm going to start bicycling to school soon, too. That's even greener.

RISING TEMPERATURES AND CHANGING OCEANS

Usually, sea turtle eggs in the lower, cooler, part of a nest become males. Eggs in the upper, warmer, part become females. Climate change is making the sand on turtle nesting beaches hotter. Hotter temperatures mean that there are many more female hatchlings than males. If there are only female sea turtles in the future, there will be no **reproduction** and no more babies. Climate change is also causing **sea levels** to rise and increasing the number and strength of storms. That is damaging and destroying beaches and the turtle nests on them. As oceans heat up, the warmer water is also destroying important places where sea turtles feed, such as coral reefs.

SPOTLIGHT ON *CORAL REEFS*

Animals called polyps make coral reefs. Coral polyps share food with a tiny algae that lives among them. Like plants, the algae produce food using energy from sunlight. The problem is they cannot do that in water that is too warm. As oceans get warmer, the algae either die or the coral ejects them, or pushes them out. The coral then starves and turns white. That is known as coral bleaching.

Since the 1950s, 50 percent of the world's coral reefs have been lost. That is a disaster for the sea turtles that live and feed on the reefs. ▶

CORAL REEFS IN DANGER

Oceans absorb some of the **carbon dioxide (CO2)** gas that is causing climate change. Too much carbon dioxide alters the chemical balance in the oceans. The water is becoming more acidic, which means it contains more acid. That makes it more difficult for corals to build the strong skeletons that form reefs. As a result, coral reefs become thinner and weaker, and they are then more likely to be broken during storms. Climate change is bringing stronger and more frequent storms. That puts coral reefs in even greater danger.

PEOPLE ON A MISSION: FIGHTING THE EFFECTS OF CLIMATE CHANGE

Many people are helping sea turtles by learning more about climate change and its effects. They are trying to find ways to save the beaches, coral reefs, and seagrass meadows on which sea turtles and many other animals rely.

Some climate and environmental scientists study how a sea level rise will affect sea turtle nests. They also figure out where they will be most affected. Rising sea levels could destroy sea turtle nesting sites around the world. Researchers have tested the impact of seawater on turtle eggs. They found that if seawater covers eggs already laid in nests, the babies inside are much less likely to hatch. Due to the increasing threat of water covering some shorelines, scientists are moving sea turtle nests to areas farther up beaches. Environment lawyers prepare cases to persuade governments that any beaches important to nesting turtles should be protected.

Scientists all around the world are also looking at how coral reefs deal with climate change. They have seen that some corals have adapted to survive in challenging conditions. They are trying to find out how. That knowledge could help conservationists restore threatened reefs back to health. It will also help preserve them as the planet continues to warm.

◀ Many people are studying the effect that climate change is having on coral reefs. They are raising awareness of the damage caused to them and the wildlife that depends on them.

31

SEA TURTLES NEED CORAL REEFS

Many sea turtles rely on coral reefs to find food. The coral reefs rely on them, too!

VEGETARIAN FEEDERS

Adult green sea turtles are mostly vegetarians. They eat seagrasses and algae from coral reefs. Green sea turtles have finely serrated, or jagged, jaws to help them scrape algae off the hard surfaces of coral.

CRUSHING JAWS

Loggerhead turtles and Kemp's ridley turtles have powerful crushing jaws. They use them to eat hard-shelled animals, such as whelks and crabs, that live among the coral reefs.

SPONGES FOR SUPPER

The hawksbill sea turtle feeds mainly on very simple animals called sponges. They live on coral reefs. The hawksbill is named for its narrow, curved, and pointed beak. It uses the beak to pick out sponges from holes in the reef. Some of the sponges are poisonous, but the turtle's body fat absorbs the poisons to keep it from getting sick.

HEALTHY CORALS

Leatherbacks and hawskbills keep sponges in check. Sponges help make up the hard structures of reefs. However, too many sponges are not healthy for coral reefs. By eating sponges, leatherback and hawksbill sea turtles play their part in keeping the reefs healthy.

33

CHAPTER FIVE

OTHER THREATS TO SEA TURTLES

The sea turtles that survive the combined threats of habitat loss, poaching, and climate change are still not safe. Sadly, these gentle ocean creatures face other threats, too.

It is estimated that more than ▶ half of the world's sea turtles have swallowed plastic or other waste.

THE PROBLEM WITH WASTE

More than 8 million tons (7.2 mt) of plastic goes in the world's oceans each year. Unlike paper or food, plastic doesn't rot for hundreds of years. Sea turtles often mistake floating plastic bags for jellyfish and can choke on them when they try and eat them. They can get entangled in fishing equipment that is lost or dumped in oceans. That can keep a sea turtle from feeding or swimming to the surface to breathe. Trash on beaches can trap hatchlings and keep them from reaching the ocean.

Kids on a Mission

 @warrior_renata_07

My family reduces, reuses, and recycles as much plastic and other items as we can. That will not only help sea turtles but all other ocean wildlife, because so much waste ends up in the ocean.

CAUGHT UP IN THE PROBLEM

Thousands of miles of nets are dropped into the oceans each day. The nets pick up almost anything in their path, so bycatch occurs every time fishing equipment is hauled in. Animals caught as bycatch are often thrown overboard, dead or dying. The main victims of bycatch are dolphins, sea turtles, and seabirds. Becoming bycatch is a huge threat to sea turtles.

▼ Experts think that by 2050, the amount of plastic in the ocean will weigh more than the amount of fish in the ocean!

" ... even one little thin, filmy piece of plastic can block a turtle's throat ... and can result in death."

Dr. Britta Hardesty, Commonwealth Scientific and Industrial Research Organisation (CSIRO)

SPOTLIGHT ON *BYCATCH*

Around the world, human populations are increasing. Every year, there are more mouths to feed. That means bigger and more efficient fishing boats are taking to the waves to catch more fish. That increases the threat of bycatch, too. In the last 50 years, hundreds of thousands of sea turtles have died after being caught in shrimp trawls, gill nets, and longline fishing gear.

SEA TURTLES IN TROUBLE

When a sea turtle gets trapped in a net or fishing line, or caught on a hook, it is unable to reach the ocean surface. Sea turtles need to get to the surface to breathe—therefore, many drown. Even if a turtle is still alive when the nets are pulled up, chances are that the turtle will have a hook left behind in its jaw, throat, or stomach. Loggerheads and leatherback sea turtles in particular often become caught in long lines.

▼ Vets in **rehabilitation** centers rescue and care for sick and injured sea turtles.

PEOPLE ON A MISSION: SEA TURTLE SCIENTISTS

Some scientists specialize in helping sea turtles. Vets work in special sea turtle hospitals that are set up along coastlines. They work with fishermen to help them save turtles caught in fishing equipment. They care for injured or sick sea turtles. If sea turtles are found alive with hooks or other fishing gear caught on them, the vets help the animals heal and then release them back into the wild.

Some scientists have come up with new inventions to help sea turtles. For example, they have designed nets with lights on them to reduce the bycatch of turtles in gill nets. Sea turtles tend to swim away from the lights, so the nets have been shown to reduce sea turtle bycatch by up to 70 percent. Some scientists specialize in working with fisheries around the world. They explain how the devices work and why they are important.

Geographic Information Systems (GIS) specialists works with GIS and other technologies to collect and study data to help wildlife and their habitats. For example, they track sea turtle movements using **satellites**. They use the information to warn fishing boats where the sea turtles are located, so the boats can avoid catching them in their nets.

▼ Sadly, this sea turtle died after becoming entangled in a fishing net.

OTHER MARINE REPTILES IN DANGER

The sea turtle is not the only ocean animal under threat. In many of Earth's oceans, other marine reptiles are also in danger.

THE SALTWATER CROCODILE

The saltwater crocodile is the largest reptile on the planet. It can grow 23 feet (6.5 m) long. It can weigh more than 2,200 pounds (1,000 kg). This dangerous predator can catch and eat just about any animal that it comes across. Saltwater crocodiles live in **mangrove** areas in the Indian Ocean and the Australian and Pacific Islands. They are threatened by habitat loss and **deforestation** in the mangroves.

THE SEA SNAKE

Sea snakes live in the tropical waters of the Pacific and Indian Oceans. Sea snakes live in coral reefs, **estuaries**, mangrove swamps, sandy shores, and the ocean. There are around 60 species of sea snakes around the world. Several are endangered due to threats that include climate change, bycatch, habitat loss, and habitat destruction. Sea snakes are also sometimes caught for their meat, skin, and internal organs. They are sometimes sold overseas, too.

THE MARINE IGUANA

Marine iguanas are the only lizards in the world that feed and live in the ocean. They swim through the water, eating algae. They also spend time lying in the sun on warm rocks. The marine iguana is found only in the Galápagos Islands. On land, cats, rats, dogs, and pigs prey, or feed on, marine iguanas. Rising sea levels and temperatures caused by climate change affect their beach-nesting habitat. The extra heat also affects the iguana's ability to control its body temperature while on land. It affects the development of its eggs, too.

39

WHAT'S NEXT FOR THE SEA TURTLE?

It's difficult to know for certain what the future holds for the world's sea turtles. There are marine reserves where sea turtles are protected from some of the threats that face them. However, many sea turtles swim far outside of these safe zones. In spite of wildlife laws, people continue to poach sea turtles. They are under threat from climate change, fishing boat nets, and pollution, too.

HELP FROM CONSERVATIONISTS

If more people work in sea turtle conservation, they can work with governments and encourage countries to sign up to international agreements that protect sea turtle **territories**.

There are already some success stories that bring hope. Sea turtles have returned to some beaches where they had disappeared. That is thanks to conservationists who have educated people about not eating turtle eggs and have worked to patrol their nesting sites. Sea turtles have also returned to beaches where tourists have been told about the risks and coastal development, including beach lighting, has been restricted.

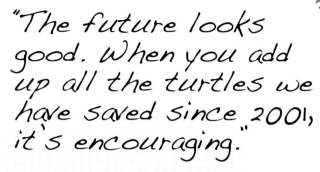

"The future looks good. When you add up all the turtles we have saved since 2001, it's encouraging."

Brandon Franklin, who works with people to alter beach lighting in Alabama

HELP FROM ORGANIZATIONS

The World Wildlife Fund (WWF) is one of the organizations fighting to save sea turtles. The WWF is working to encourage governments to make stronger laws that protect sea turtles and their reserves. That includes better training for law enforcement officers. The WWF is working to increase the number of turtle conservationists in many parts of the world. These conservationists monitor and patrol turtle nests. They are helping local communities set up **ecotourism** services that offer ways to earn money instead of poaching.

Kids on a Mission

@turtlekid_2006

I asked my family to avoid buying seafood or choose responsibly caught seafood instead. This seafood is caught in ways that avoid bycatch and help keep sea turtles and other sea animals safe.

HELP FROM ALL OF US

We can all play our part in helping to save the sea turtle. We can take actions to limit climate change, from switching to energy efficient light bulbs to taking the bus instead of a car. We can read all we can about sea turtles and tell our friends and family what we have learned. There are already signs that some sea turtle populations are recovering. If we all work together, we can save the spectacular sea turtle.

MAKE IT YOUR MISSION: A CAREER IN CONSERVATION

Why not make it your mission to build a future career in conservation? That way, you could make a huge difference to sea turtles and other endangered animals. On pages 44–45, you'll find some of the conservation careers that you could pursue. And here are things you can do right now to prepare for a career in conservation and help save sea turtles.

GET SET TO STUDY

If you want a career in conservation, work hard at school now. Pay attention in your science, English, and geography classes. Languages are also useful. If you get a job overseas, being able to speak a foreign language will be very helpful.

GET CONNECTED

Getting involved with a conservation group or charity can be really satisfying. You'll find some of the organizations you can join on page 47. Getting to know other people who are concerned about wildlife is a great way to find out what you can do to help endangered animals. Being involved with conservation organizations and charities now will also help you when you apply for jobs in the future. It will show that you have been interested in conservation from an early age.

▼ If you adopt a sea turtle through the WWF, the money you pay will go toward protecting sea turtles and their habitats.

TAKE ACTION!

You have learned about some of the actions that help sea turtles from the Kids on a Mission features in this book. Here are some more ideas for other activities that can help protect sea turtles:

- Adopt a sea turtle! Ask your parents to help you check out the WWF site for information about adopting sea turtles.
- Jellyfish are one of a sea turtle's favorite foods, but jellyfish look a lot like plastic bags. So, bring your own reusable bags when you shop to keep more plastic bags from ending up in oceans.
- Join in or organize beach cleanups. Removing litter from beaches ensures it doesn't get into the oceans and endanger the wildlife there.
- Ask your school to hold a fundraising event to raise money for an organization such as the WWF and help it protect sea turtles.
- Start a blog about sea turtles and the dangers they face. Educate as many people as you can.

GET EXPERIENCE

It is important to get some work experience if you want a career in conservation. Any form of work experience in wildlife care will help you decide the best way of using your talents in a future conservation career. Working for local zoos, charities, and conservation organizations as soon as you can will help give you the skills you need, too.

Cleaning litter from your local ▶ environment will help protect animals and their habitats.

CAREERS IN CONSERVATION

Conservation is a huge growth area today, as more and more people turn their focus to concerns about the environment. There are a huge number of conservation jobs available. Here is information about just some of them. You can find out about other conservation jobs on page 47 of this book.

▲ If you're someone who likes being outdoors and getting your hands dirty, a wildlife manager could be the job for you.

WILDLIFE ECONOMIST

If you're good at math, perhaps you could become a wildlife economist. In this job, you would figure out the economic benefits of wildlife to individuals, as well as local and national businesses and governments. You could study the facts and figures related to tourist visits to marine reserves and find out what the economic benefits to sea turtle habitats are. This important job can make a huge difference to conservation decisions.

WILDLIFE MANAGER

Wildlife managers look after the animals in a natural area. In this role, you would monitor poaching in a habitat. You would also keep track of the animal populations in the area and ensure that the habitat is suitable for the wildlife. You might also collect data and prepare research to help conservationists make decisions about how to help wildlife. A degree in environmental studies is usually needed.

WILDLIFE CONSULTANT

A wildlife consultant is a scientist who conducts research and surveys to provide advice on environmental issues. In this role, you might look at how plans to use a particular area of beach may affect the sea turtles that nest nearby, for example. You could also create habitat restoration plans and check how successful they are when in place. Most wildlife consultants are wildlife biologists, so you would need a degree in biology.

PUBLIC RELATIONS OFFICER

If you like raising awareness about important issues, this could be the role for you. Public relations officers manage communications between organizations and the public. In this job, you could work for charities, wildlife organizations, and governments. You would raise awareness of wildlife issues. A degree in marketing is useful.

ENVIRONMENTAL SCIENTIST

If you become an environmental scientist, you will often gather information in the field. You may also conduct lab tests. For example, you might analyze water to check for pollution. You might test water to find the type, amount, and source of the pollution. An environmental science degree is usually required.

ENVIRONMENTAL LAWYER

Some environmental lawyers work for companies. In this role, you would advise the companies about the possible environmental effects they are having. That might include pollution they are causing through their practices, for example. If you worked for the government, you would help write laws that protect the environment and take people to court for breaking those laws. If you want to become an environmental lawyer, you will need a law degree with a specialization in environmental law.

◀ If you're good at science and would like to do something to help the world's wildlife and habitats, then you could consider training to be an environmental scientist.

GLOSSARY

adapted changed to deal with new conditions

algae plantlike organisms that grow in damp places

algal blooms rapid growths of algae

aquariums buildings containing tanks of live fish, sea turtles, and other ocean species

atmosphere the blanket of gases that surrounds Earth

befouling making dirty or polluted

carbon dioxide (CO2) a gas that contributes to climate change when released into the atmosphere

climate change a shift in the average weather conditions on Earth

communications the sharing of messages or information

conservation protection of the planet

conservationists people who try and protect the planet

coral reefs structures in the ocean made up of thousands of tiny animals called coral polyps

critically endangered facing an extremely high risk of extinction in the wild

crustaceans animals that usually have a hard covering or shell and two pairs of feelers

deforestation cutting down large areas of trees in a forest

ecotourism tourism that has little negative impact on the environment

endangered facing a very high risk of extinction in the wild

environment a natural place where plants and animals live

erosion the wearing away of soil and rock, usually by wind, water, or ice

estuaries areas where freshwater rivers meet salty oceans

extinct died out

fertilizers substances that help plants grow

fossil fuels fuels formed from the remains of plants and animals that lived long ago

geological related to Earth's structure

Global Positioning System (GPS) a system of satellites in space that tells us were something is

habitats places in which plants and animals live

hatchlings baby animals that have just hatched from eggs

magnetic field an area where magnetic forces occur

mangrove a tree or shrub that grows in tropical coastal areas

marine reserves protected areas of ocean

mollusks animals with a soft body that are usually covered with a shell

organisms living things such as plants and animals

pesticides substances used to kill insects that harm plants and farm crops

pollution substances that are harmful to living things

populations all the people who are living in certain areas

reflects bounces back off

rehabilitation restoring an animal back to health

reproduction the act of producing babies or young

reptile a type of animal that includes snakes, lizards, crocodiles, turtles, and tortoises

satellites objects in space that orbit, or circle, bigger objects

sea anemones small, brightly colored sea animals that look a little like flowers

seagrass a grasslike plant that lives in or close to the oceans

sea levels the average levels of the surface of the ocean

sense related to the five senses of sight, hearing, smell, taste, and touch

species a type of plant or animal

sustainable can be relied upon for the forseeable future

territories areas of land that an animal regards as its own and that it may defend from other animals

trade the exchange of goods for money

FIND OUT MORE

BOOKS

Gish, Melissa. *Sea Turtle* (Spotlight on Nature). Creative Paperbacks, 2019.

Hestermann, Bethanie and Josh. *The Fascinating Ocean Book for Kids: 500 Incredible Facts!* (Fascinating Facts). Rockridge Press, 2021.

Modany, Angela. *Animal Encyclopedia: 2,500 Animals with Photos, Maps, and More!* (National Geographic Kids). National Geographic Kids, 2021.

WEBSITES

Discover more about careers that help fight climate change at:
www.bestcolleges.com/blog/climate-change-jobs

Discover the ultimate guide to careers in conservation at:
www.conservation-careers.com/15-key-conservation-jobs-ultimate-guide-for-conservation-job-seekers

Hear directly from people working in conservation. Find out what they have to say about a career in conservation at:
www.conservation-careers.com/conservation-jobs-careers-advice/how-to-get-a-job-in-conservation

Find out more about sea turtle conservation at:
https://conserveturtles.org/information-about-sea-turtles-an-introduction

Learn more about sea turtles and their watery world at:
https://ocean.si.edu/ocean-life/reptiles/sea-turtles

Find lots of amazing wildlife careers and what they involve at this useful site:
www.thebalancecareers.com/careers-with-wildlife-125918

Discover what the world's leading wildlife organization, the WWF, is doing to help sea turtles and how you can get involved:
www.worldwildlife.org/species/sea-turtle

Publisher's note to educators and parents:
All the websites featured above have been carefully reviewed to ensure that they are suitable for students. However, many websites change often, and we cannot guarantee that a site's future contents will continue to meet our high standards of educational value. Please be advised that students should be closely monitored whenever they access the Internet.

INDEX

ABOUT THE AUTHOR

Award-winning author Louise Spilsbury, who also writes under the name Louise Kay Stewart, has written over 250 books for young people on a wide range of exciting subjects. She especially loves writing about animals and learning more about what we can all do to protect amazing species such as the sea turtle.